LIGHTNING BOLT BOOKS™

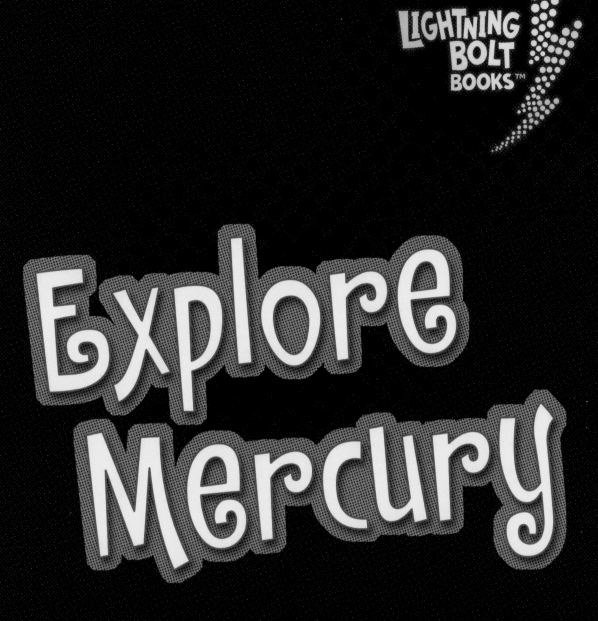

Explore Mercury

Liz Milroy

Lerner Publications ◆ Minneapolis

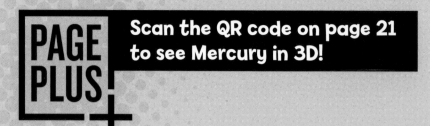

Scan the QR code on page 21 to see Mercury in 3D!

Lerner Publications Company
An imprint of Lerner Publishing Group, Inc.
241 First Avenue North
Minneapolis, MN 55401 USA

For reading levels and more information, look up this title at www.lernerbooks.com.

Main body text set in Billy Infant regular.
Typeface provided by SparkType.

Editor: Brianna Kaiser

Library of Congress Cataloging-in-Publication Data

Names: Milroy, Liz, author.
Title: Explore Mercury / Liz Milroy.
Other titles: Lightning bolt books. Planet explorer.
Description: Minneapolis, MN : Lerner Publications, [2021] | Series: Lightning bolt books - Planet explorer | Includes bibliographical references and index. | Audience: Ages 6–9 | Audience: Grades 2–3 | Summary: "Did you know Mercury doesn't have any moons? In this energetic text, readers will get a glimpse of interesting facts and scientific explanations about what makes Mercury unique"— Provided by publisher.
Identifiers: LCCN 2020016127 (print) | LCCN 2020016128 (ebook) | ISBN 9781728404110 (library binding) | ISBN 9781728423630 (paperback) | ISBN 9781728418476 (ebook)
Subjects: LCSH: Mercury (Planet)—Juvenile literature.
Classification: LCC QB611 .M55 2021 (print) | LCC QB611 (ebook) | DDC 523.41—dc23

LC record available at https://lccn.loc.gov/2020016127
LC ebook record available at https://lccn.loc.gov/2020016128

Manufactured in the United States of America
1-48469-48983-6/11/2020

Table of Contents

All about Mercury

The sun would look much bigger than you've ever seen it if you were on Mercury. Mercury is the smallest planet in our solar system.

Mercury Venus Earth Mars Jupiter Saturn Uranus Neptune

This diagram shows the order of the planets in the solar system.

Mercury is the closest planet to the sun. Mercury is about 36 million miles (58 million km) from the sun.

Like Earth, Venus, and Mars, Mercury is called a rocky planet. Rocky planets are smaller than other kinds of planets and are mostly solid.

Left to right: Earth, Mars, Venus, and Mercury are the rocky planets in our solar system.

This image shows how small Mercury is compared to Earth.

Mercury is 3,030 miles (4,878 km) across. A little more than eighteen Mercurys could fit inside Earth.

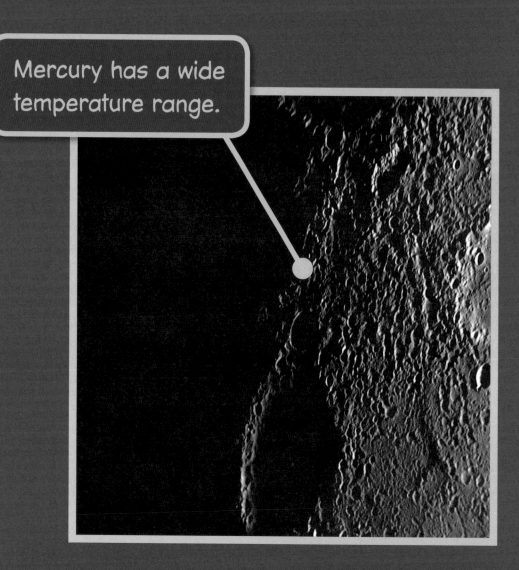

Mercury has a wide temperature range.

Mercury is superhot during the day, but at night it can get very cold. Temperatures can reach up to 800°F (425°C) and drop as low as -290°F (-180°C).

Mercury might be closest to the sun, but it is not the hottest planet in our solar system. Venus has a thick atmosphere that traps heat. This keeps it hotter than its neighbors.

Mercury's neighbor Venus is the hottest planet in the solar system.

What's in a Name?

Ancient people noticed that Mercury moved more quickly across the sky than other planets. They named it after the Roman god Mercury. He was the speedy messenger of the gods.

Mercury is also the name of a chemical. In the past, people made thermometers, batteries, and other things with mercury.

The chemical Mercury used to be used in thermometers.

Living on Mercury

On Mercury, the days are long, but the years are short. One day is as long as almost fifty-nine Earth days. A year takes only eighty-eight Earth days.

Mercury's atmosphere is very thin.

There is not much air on Mercury because it has a really thin atmosphere. If people landed there, they would not be able to breathe.

Mercury doesn't have seasons. Earth does because it is tilted on an axis, but Mercury is barely tilted.

This shows Mercury's tilt compared to those of the other planets.

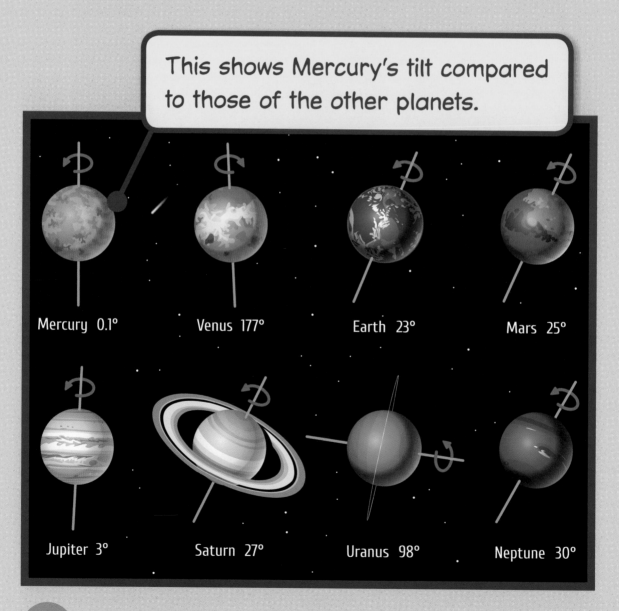

Mercury 0.1°   Venus 177°   Earth 23°   Mars 25°

Jupiter 3°   Saturn 27°   Uranus 98°   Neptune 30°

The sun appears bigger from Mercury than it does from Earth.

From Mercury, the sun looks very big and moves strangely. Sometimes it even moves backward. If people could live on Mercury, they would see the sun rise and set only three times in six years.

Checking Out Mercury

Astronomers sent spacecraft to visit Mercury twice. The first to explore Mercury was *Mariner 10* in 1974. It flew by Mercury three times.

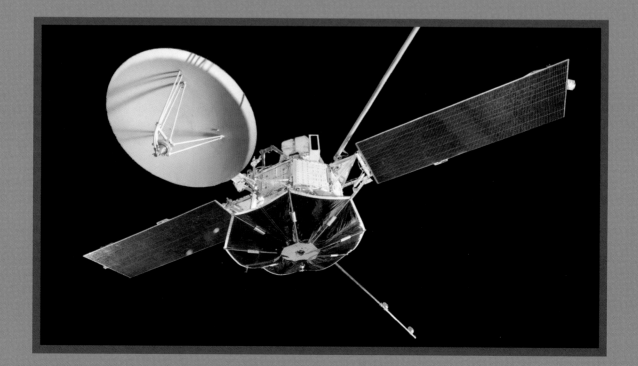

This is a photo of Mercury taken by *Mariner 10*.

Mariner 10 also explored Venus. It was the first spacecraft to explore two planets in one mission.

The second spacecraft, *MESSENGER*, was the first to orbit Mercury. It orbited Mercury from 2011 to 2015.

MESSENGER near Mercury's surface

A spacecraft flies near Mercury.

In 2018, two spacecraft in the mission *BepiColombo* left Earth for Mercury. They will study Mercury's surface and interior and will enter Mercury's orbit in 2025. Keep an eye out for news about our small neighbor.

Planet Facts

- Mercury is so close to the sun that it can be seen from Earth only right before sunrise and after sunset. Some ancient people thought it was two different planets.

- The surface of Mercury looks a lot like our moon because both have many craters. Mercury's craters are named after famous artists, musicians, and authors, including Dr. Seuss.

- The biggest moon in our solar system, Ganymede, is bigger than Mercury. Ganymede orbits Jupiter.

Space Story

People used to think that one side of Mercury always faced the sun. They couldn't see if Mercury was spinning. In 1965, scientists bounced a radio signal off of it. They saw that Mercury does spin. But it spins very slowly. Mercury travels almost 150 million miles (241 million km) in the time it takes to turn around once.

Scan the QR code to the right to see Mercury in 3D!

Glossary

astronomer: a scientist who looks at stars, planets, and other things in outer space

atmosphere: a layer of gas that surrounds a planet

axis: an invisible line that Mercury turns around

orbit: the path taken by one body circling around another body

rocky planet: also called a terrestrial planet, a rocky planet is made up of mostly rocks or metals. Mercury, Venus, Earth, and Mars are all rocky planets.

solar system: our sun and everything that orbits around it

spacecraft: a ship made by people to move through space

year: the amount of time it takes for a planet to orbit its sun once

Learn More

Beth, Georgia. *Discover Mercury*. Minneapolis: Lerner Publications, 2019.

Milroy, Liz. *Explore Jupiter*. Minneapolis: Lerner Publications, 2021.

NASA for Students
https://www.nasa.gov/stem/forstudents/k-4/index.html

NASA Space Place—All about Mercury
https://spaceplace.nasa.gov/all-about-mercury/en/

Nichols, Michelle. *Astronomy Lab for Kids: 52 Family-Friendly Activities*. Beverly, MA: Quarry, 2016.

Ready, Jet, Go! Planets in Our Solar System
https://pbskids.org/learn/readyjetgo/

Index

Photo Acknowledgments

Image credits: NASA/JHUAPL, p. 4; WP/Wikimedia Commons (CC BY-SA 3.0), p. 5; Lsmpascal/Wikimedia Commons (CC BY-SA 3.0), p. 6; NASA/APL (from MESSENGER), p. 7; NASA/Johns Hopkins University Applied Physics Laboratory/Carnegie Institution of Washington, pp. 8, 12, 13, 18; NASA/Goddard Space Flight Center Conceptual Image Lab, p. 9; Bequest of Phyllis Massar, 2011/Metropolitan Museum of Art (CC0 1.0), p. 10; Anonimski/Wikimedia Commons (CC BY-SA 3.0), p. 11; Vera Serg/Shutterstock.com, p. 14; NASA/SDO/AIA/Goddard Space Flight Center, p. 15; Eric Long/Smithsonian National Air and Space Museum (NASM2019-01580) (CC0 1.0), p. 16; NASA/JPL, pp. 17, 19.

Cover: NASA/Messenger team, Jason Harwell.